Alexander the Great

Pocket **BIOGRAPHIES**

Alexander the Great

E.E. RICE

SUTTON PUBLISHING

First published in 1997 by
Sutton Publishing Limited · Phoenix Mill
Thrupp · Stroud · Gloucestershire · GL5 2BU

British Library Cataloguing in Publication Data
A catalogue record for this book is available from the British
Library.

ISBN 0-7509-1528-5

™ ALAN SUTTON™ and SUTTON™ are the trade
marks of Sutton Publishing Limited

Typeset in 13/18 pt Perpetua.
Typesetting and origination by
Sutton Publishing Limited.
Printed in Great Britain by
The Guernsey Press Company Limited
Guernsey, Channel Islands.

In Memoriam
Betty Nye Quinn
Professor of Classics,
Mount Holyoke College

obiit 29 January 1997

CONTENTS

CHRONOLOGY

356 BC	Birth of Alexander the Great in Macedonia
338 BC	King Philip II of Macedonia defeats allied Greek armies at Chaironeia
336 BC	First invasion of Asia; King Philip assassinated at Aigai; accession of Alexander to the Macedonian throne
335 BC	Alexander's campaigns in Thrace and Illyria; the destruction of Thebes
334 BC	Alexander begins his invasion of the Persian Empire; the Battle of the Granicus river; the sieges of Miletus and Halicarnassus
334–3 BC	Conquest of southern Asia Minor; visit to Gordion near Ankara
333 BC	The Battle of Issus
332 BC	The siege and capture of Tyre and Gaza
332–1 BC	Alexander conquers Egypt, founds Alexandria, and visits the Oracle of Ammon at the Siwah Oasis
331 BC	The Battle of Gaugamela
330 BC	The burning of Persepolis; death of the Persian Great King Darius III; murders of Philotas and Parmenio

Chronology

329–8 BC	Campaigns in Bactria and Sogdiana; the capture of Bessus; the murder of Cleitus; the Royal Pages' Conspiracy; the arrest of Callisthenes; the revolt and death of Spitamenes
327 BC	Alexander marries Rhoxane; the invasion of India
326–5 BC	The Battle of the Hydaspes against Porus; the mutiny on the Hyphasis river; the voyage down the Indus; the campaign against the Malli
325 BC	The march across the Gedrosian desert
324 BC	The mass marriage at Susa; the mutiny at Opis; the death of Hephaistion
323 BC	The death of Alexander the Great at Babylon

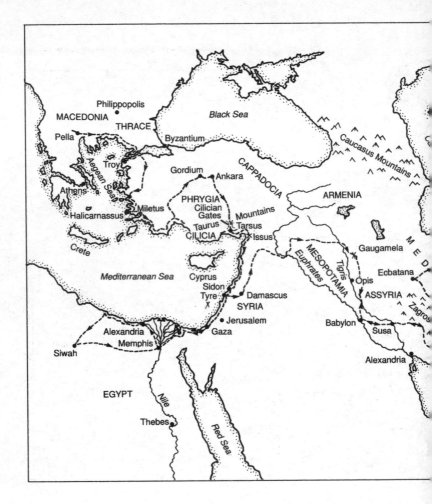

Alexander's progress --→-------→---

Aral
Sea

Alexandria Eschate

Maracanda

Hindu Kush

Aornus

Indus

Bactra
BACTRIA

Hydaspes

PARTHIA

Caspian Gates

hran

Khyber
Pass

Toxila
Nicaea

Bucephala

Alexandria
in Aria

ARACHOSIA

Malli

Acesines

Hydraotes

Hyphasis

Pasargadae

untains

Alexandria in
Arachosia

Alexandria Opiana

Persepolis

PERSIS

CARMANIA

GEDROSIA

INDIA

ersian
Gates

Gedrosian
Desert

Indus

Persian Gulf

Strait of Hormuz

Alexander's Port

INTRODUCTION
AND SOURCES

It is a daunting task to write a biography of Alexander the Great. In the first place there is much that is not known about one of the most famous figures in history. In the second place, the heavily documented scholarly bibliography which already exists – due in part to the endless speculation caused by our lack of information – is huge and constantly growing. In this Pocket Biography I have therefore attempted to present a short account of Alexander's life based on a synthesis of academic material known to me, which is aimed at the intelligent general reader interested in the facts and problems which I and other ancient historians think are important to the understanding of this enigmatic figure. Of necessity I have had to be ruthlessly selective within the confines of this series and would never claim that this book is comprehensive or intended to be so. It is emphatically not a documented account of Alexander's military campaigns. I hope none the less that this volume may go some way to dispel various myths commonly held about Alexander by those who have not had the opportunity to delve behind the many strictly 'popular' writings about him which exist.

The Sources

That we know anything at all about Alexander is primarily due to the ancient literary sources which discuss him. Many university students in my experience would gladly pass over a section on 'source criticism', the analytical study of historical sources to determine the worth of what any of them say. However, this is an essential part of the study of history, and the study of Alexander poses a major source problem. Many, many histories of Alexander were written in antiquity (he was a source of fascination to the ancients as well as to moderns), but most are known only by title or in fragments because of the circumstances of historical survival. These included eyewitness accounts by men who had accompanied Alexander's expedition (the so-called 'primary sources'), who were at least in a position to tell the truth about the parts of the campaigns they knew about *in so far as they understood it*, although bias or even malice might have crept in. A notable example was Callisthenes of Olynthus (a Greek city in Chalkidiki in Macedonia), a relative of the philosopher Aristotle, who accompanied Alexander's expedition as its official historian. It is often said that 'he was the Homer to Alexander's Achilles' (a reference to the epic poem the *Iliad* which celebrated the Trojan War and the Greek hero Achilles, by a poet traditionally known as Homer). There were also later writers who both made use of these eyewitness accounts and drew upon the wealth of popular stories which quickly grew up about Alexander.

The most reliable of the latter group (so-called 'secondary sources') form the basis of all modern histories of Alexander the Great. The best known of these writers is Lucius Flavius Arrianus, 'Arrian' in anglicised form, who was a Greek from the Roman province of Bithynia (an area of modern Turkey near the south-west corner of the Black Sea). Arrian was a prolific historical writer with a busy and successful political career in the Roman civil service. Although his exact dates continue to be debated, he lived in the last decade or so of the first century AD throughout the first decades or more of the second century; that is, more than four hundred years after Alexander's death, and therefore without any personal knowledge of his subject. His six-book history of Alexander is known in Greek as the *Anabasis* (literally 'an expedition up into a country'), and provides a coherent, chronological, and largely convincing description of Alexander's campaigns. Arrian states that he based his history on two main eyewitness accounts available to him: that of Ptolemy, Alexander's boyhood friend in Macedonia and later a general (subequently to become King Ptolemy I of Egypt), and that of a man named Aristoboulos, usually considered a civil engineer of some kind. We do not know why Arrian chose these sources nor how good they were. Since other Alexander historians do not use them, we have no independent evidence for their worth or otherwise. He also includes various 'stories' or 'tales' (as he calls them) about Alexander, the origin of which remains obscure. Much of the difficulty in interpreting Arrian arises from this lack of knowledge about his sources. Arrian has been criticised in many areas, but despite the problems of his sources and his late date, his *Anabasis* appears to be our best history of Alexander. Arrian also wrote a separate work called the *Indika* ('Indian Matters') which described the journey of part of Alexander's army down the Indus river and along the Persian Gulf in 325–4 BC. This was based on the account of Alexander's admiral Nearchus who headed the expedition.

The second important secondary source for Alexander is Diodorus Siculus ('Siculus' is the Latin adjective meaning 'Sicilian'). Diodorus wrote during the first century BC a work translated from the Greek as the *Historical Library*. This was a chronological history of the world from mythological times until his own day. Necessarily generalised and brief, this type of historical writing enjoyed considerable popularity in Roman times, in the same way as encyclopaedias can be used today instead of detailed books on individual topics. Book XVII of this work contains a history of Alexander the Great. Living so much later and facing a task of enormous scope, Diodorus was clearly dependent on earlier sources for his material, but in Book XVII he does not identify them (or it). This question has occasioned considerable debate and the answer may never be known for certain, but most scholars, using a combination of complex arguments, consider as his main source a shadowy historian by the name of Cleitarchus, who is known to have written *Histories of Alexander* in at least twelve books. Whether or not this is true, Diodorus's account has similarities to other histories of Alexander, and together these works are known as the 'vulgate tradition', characterised by a colourful, rhetorical, and less critical narrative. The significance of Diodorus and the vulgate tradition is that it gives a very different picture from that later found in Arrian, and scholars must try to reconcile the two.

The third major source comes from the field of biography rather than history. Plutarch, a Greek of the second century AD from Boiotia in central Greece, composed among his voluminous writings a series of *Parallel Lives of Greeks and Romans*, in which biographies of famous figures from Greek and Roman history were paired in order to provide a moral lesson for the reader. His *Life of Alexander* was twinned with that of Julius Caesar. Plutarch states in the introduction that he is writing 'lives' not 'histories', and the result is a strikingly different

narrative style. Within a general chronological
framework of Alexander's life, Plutarch includes
incidents and anecdotes which he judges to be
illustrative of his subject's character. To achieve this,
Plutarch uses sources liberally, and quotes them.
Not surprisingly, these are often sources not found
in the 'proper' historians of Alexander: to take but
one example, the royal chamberlain Chares, who
was in a position to reveal details of Alexander's
personal habits behind the scenes. The result is an
immensely readable, circumstantial account,
studded with colourful anecdotes not found
elsewhere which concentrate on Alexander the man
rather than Alexander the king and conqueror. It is
not surprising that modern biographers and
novelists have frequently drawn heavily on Plutarch
for material to flesh out their picture of a fascinating
figure otherwise known primarily on the battlefield
or in the camp. The historical worth of Plutarch's
mostly uncorroborated information is, however,
quite another question.

In addition to Arrian, Diodorus, and Plutarch,
the most prominent minor literary source is the
Latin history of Alexander by one Quintus Curtius
Rufus, whose identity, date, and purpose in writing

are alike unknown. Although it clearly belongs to the vulgate tradition, the interpretation of the text has been hampered by its relation to the genre of Roman rhetorical writing, and the problems have been endlessly debated. Also to be considered are real or fictional letters of Alexander (quoted variously by the Alexander historians), the so-called 'Journals' of Alexander the Great (the explanation of which is still uncertain, but which may be a bogus document designed to muddy the waters surrounding Alexander's death), and the *Alexander Romance*, a fictitious and fantastic account of Alexander's life which has more in common with the ancient novel and medieval romances.

THE EARLY YEARS

The Macedonian Background

In antiquity Macedonia was a large region of northern Greece, not to be confused with the province of that name in modern Greece, nor with the former Yugoslav republic of Macedonia. The heartland may be thought of as the lowland area formed by river valleys flowing into the Thermaic Gulf (this area now includes the modern city of Thessaloniki, which was not founded until 316 BC, after the death of Alexander). At its greatest extent in the fourth century BC, in the east Macedonia encompassed the three-pronged Chalkidiki peninsula and lands as far as Thrace and the Black Sea, in the south it stretched as far as Thessaly, in the west across the Pindus mountains (the highest mountain range of Greece, which divides northern Greece down the middle) into modern Albania, and in the north it covered much of the former Yugoslav republics and parts of Bulgaria. It was a vast territory, geographically diverse, rich in natural resources, and encompassing various tribal peoples.

Macedonia was a kingdom ruled throughout classical times by a hereditary kingship in which the strongest contender assumed the crown. As such, it was politically distinct from the city-states of Greece in the south, although there had been contacts between Macedonia and Greece for hundreds of years: Greek cities had been founded along the east coast of Macedonia and in Chalkidiki, and recent archaeological excavation has made it clear that the rich culture at least of the aristocratic class in Macedonia was as sophisticated as any found further south. At the beginning of the fourth century a new capital city was founded at Pella (west of modern Thessaloniki), and it was here that the famous Greek tragedian Euripides spent his last years. Remarkable mosaic pavements, villas, the market area, and now the palace have been found (as I write, the finds from the market and palace have not yet been fully published), testifying to a rich, cultivated and sophisticated society completely familiar with the culture of Greece. None the less, there was a deep ethnic rivalry between Greeks and

Macedonians, which the political hostilities between them did nothing to dispel.

Alexander's father, Philip II, was the greatest fourth-century king of Macedonia. It was he who united many of the warlike tribes in northern and western Macedonia, exploited the vast natural resources of silver and gold to enrich his treasury, and forged the Macedonian army into a lethal fighting force which his son later used to deadly effect. Although his principal queen (and Alexander's mother) was Olympias, a princess of Epirus (a land lying across the Pindus mountains to the west), Philip made a series of polygamous marriages which reinforced a nexus of guest-friendships and alliances with his neighbours. King Philip's autocratic power and expansionist tendencies were feared by the cities of mainland Greece. We see this clearly through the powerful rhetoric of the Athenian orator Demosthenes, many of whose famous speeches warned the Greeks of the danger posed to their democratic governments by Philip. Their fear was well-founded: Philip decisively defeated the combined forces of the Greeks at the battle of Chaironeia in central Greece in 338 BC, and thereby, to all intents and purposes, became the arbiter of Greek affairs. The young Alexander played a notable part in this battle as his father's lieutenant.

In a move typical of his cunning diplomacy, Philip controlled the fractious Greeks through the so-called League of Corinth, a loose federation of cities in an unequal alliance with him without any basis of goodwill or friendship. At the initial meeting held at Corinth, Philip obtained the agreement of the cities to support him in a war against Persia, and he was elected supreme commander of the allied Greek forces for this expedition. It is not clear what Philip's actual intentions were regarding Persia, but the pretext for the invasion, calculated to appeal to the mainland Greeks, was the liberation of the Greek cities of Asia Minor from the yoke of Persian oppression. There had been a deep-seated hostility between Greece and Persia since the days of the Persian War in the early fifth century BC (immortalised by the historian Herodotus). The impetus for that war had been the revolt of the Greek cities of Asia Minor against Persia, and the idea of the 'freedom of the Greeks' under Persian rule had been a powerful rallying cry ever since. An advance force under the Macedonian generals Parmenio and Attalus reached the Hellespont, but was besieged at Perinthus. The expedition was thrown into further confusion by the assassination of Philip II in 336 BC.

Back in the old royal capital of Aigai (modern Vergina), Philip had been presiding at the wedding of his daughter Cleopatra, Alexander's full sister, to her royal Epirot uncle, when he was killed in the theatre by a youth with a personal grievance (allegedly romantic) against him. Philip was buried at Aigai in accordance with royal tradition. Convincing forensic investigations have shown beyond reasonable doubt that he was the occupant of the main chamber of Tomb II in the royal tumulus of Vergina, discovered in 1979 (the woman's body in the ante-chamber is thought to be that of his last wife, also called Cleopatra). As one of the very few unplundered royal tombs known from ancient Greece, this tomb contained staggering riches of gold, silver and ivory which completely altered our understanding of fourth-century Macedonian culture. (These tombs at Vergina are now open to the public, and the finds are displayed in the Archaeological Museum at Thessaloniki. The theatre in which Philip was probably killed has been uncovered on the hill below the fourth-century palace at Vergina.)

Alexander's Youth

Thus at the age of twenty the young prince Alexander was unexpectedly left fatherless and the kingdom leaderless. Let us review what is known about his early life.

Alexander was born in 356 BC (possibly in the palace at Pella or the one at Aigai/Vergina) as the first son of Philip II and his queen, Olympias. The sources depict Olympias as a formidable woman with a fearsome temper who was attracted to religious rites centring on the cult of Dionysus, the Greek god of wine and much else besides, who was worshipped in an unrestrained manner in Macedonia. Olympias was determined that Alexander should succeed to the throne, and she was fiercely protective of his position at court, especially in relation to the illegitimate children sired by Philip. Alexander appears to have inherited his mother's strength of character, and he remained close to her throughout his life. (She guarded his authority in Macedonia throughout his absence during the expedition, and various sources tell of letters written between them in those years.)

Alexander spent his early years in the company of the 'royal pages', boys from aristocratic families who were brought to court for an education (along with sons of Philip's allies who, by their very presence under his eye, were virtually hostages). Many of these boyhood companions became officers under Alexander later, such as Ptolemy, son of Lagus (the historical source used by Arrian), and Nearchus, who would become the admiral of the fleet.

Tradition maintains that Philip hired as tutor for his young son the famous philosopher Aristotle, a Greek from the city of Stagira in Chalkidiki. Aristotle is said by Plutarch to have taught Alexander at the Sanctuary of the Nymphs at Mieza, where the stone seats and shady walks were still visible in his own day. This sanctuary has been identified to the north-west of the modern town Beroia (not far from the Great Tomb of Lefkadia). Archaeological excavation is incomplete, but the beautiful wooded, well-watered sanctuary appeals to the imagination as a place suited to the school of Aristotle (see plate 4). Much is often made of the philosophical influence that Aristotle had on his young charge. Opinions range from the minimum to the extreme hypothesis that Alexander's expedition was largely a scientific field trip on Aristotle's behalf. The latter view is based on a certainly fictitious letter from Alexander to Aristotle, preserved in some 'vulgate' sources, in which he writes to his tutor about some of the unusual flora and fauna he encountered on his journeys. The truth is probably somewhere in between and will never be known. That Alexander's expedition revealed a host of natural curiosities I do not doubt; that it was the primary focus of it I cannot believe. Later ancient writers, followed by certain modern scholars, have speculated about the influence of philosophical instruction on Alexander's character (the concept of 'a good king', the virtue of moderation, etc.), but without reaching many useful conclusions.

Various charming anecdotes about Alexander's early life are preserved in Plutarch, illuminating Alexander's precocious nature, intelligence and love of learning, bravery, and undoubted destiny to rule. One of the most famous incidents illustrating all the above traits concerns the taming of the horse Bucephalas (the name in Greek means 'Ox-head'). This untamable steed was offered for purchase to

King Philip, but as none could control him the king ordered the horse to be led away. After much pleading by Alexander, the boy was allowed to try to tame him, the price of his failure being the forfeit of the price of the horse. Alexander had noticed that the horse appeared to shy at his own shadow, and led him directly into the sun so that it was invisible. He was thereby able to calm the beast, and eventually to mount and ride him when all others had failed. Bucephalas later accompanied his master as far as India, where he died, to Alexander's considerable grief. All the sources record Alexander's devotion to the animal, and he is said to have founded in India a city named Bucephala in its honour.

Alexander grew up as Philip's heir-apparent, serving with him on military expeditions and acting as regent in the king's absence. However, the bad feeling which had grown up between King Philip and Olympias because of his subsequent marriages and illegitimate children culminated in a major quarrel on the occasion of Philip's last marriage to Cleopatra (sometimes called Eurydice), niece of the Macedonian general Attalus. At a drunken gathering Alexander overheard Attalus invoking divine aid for a legitimate successor to be born from this union. Alexander exploded in fury. Philip drew a sword against him but was prevented by drunkenness from attacking his son. After this incident, Alexander and Olympias were exiled from court (she to Epirus, he to Illyria), along with several of Alexander's companions.

After Philip's murder, the exiles returned to Macedonia, and Alexander took steps to establish himself firmly upon his father's throne. Many have suspected that Alexander had been involved behind the scenes in the murder of Philip, mainly on the grounds that he was the primary beneficiary of the crime, but no evidence has been found for this allegation. Alexander killed or had killed his main rivals for the throne, including a royal cousin. Such power struggles were typical of the Macedonian royal succession, in which the strongest claimant gained the prize. Olympias oversaw the murder of Philip's wife Cleopatra and her baby daughter. Prince Alexander was now King Alexander III of Macedonia.

Alexander took over where his father had left off regarding the Greeks and the expedition against Persia. In 335 BC, he convened a meeting of the members of the League of Corinth, and persuaded them to elect him their Supreme Commander in a war of revenge against Persia, exactly as Philip had done two years previously. All the Greeks agreed to this with the exception of Sparta, a slight which rankled. Before he could turn his attention to Persia, Alexander had to secure his position in Europe. In the course of successfully quelling the revolts which had erupted among native tribes in Illyria, Thrace, and on the Danube at the news of Philip's death (covered in detail in Book I of Arrian's *Anabasis*), Alexander grew into a mature general, his campaigns in this hostile territory marked by the tactical and strategic brilliance which is manifest throughout his career.

In Alexander's absence a revolt broke out in Greece. The city of Thebes in Boiotia in central Greece had been occupied by a Macedonian garrison since the Battle of Chaironeia in 338, and disaffected exiles expelled from Thebes returned by invitation from within, killed the garrison commanders, and incited the populace to rebel against their occupiers, claiming that Alexander had been killed in the north. Alexander took this threat seriously and marched south to Thebes. This action illustrates the basic Macedonian distrust of Greeks which is evident throughout Alexander's reign, and stemmed from the feelings of ethnic rivalry and hostility which had developed during the fourth century. Arrian tells us in the context of the Theban revolt that Alexander had long been suspicious of Athens, and decided to deal with Thebes lest other Greek states, including Sparta, join in a revolutionary movement against him. We will see this atmosphere of mistrust time and time again.

Alexander's siege of Thebes is a famous episode which is related in all our sources, although the details vary. The Macedonian army arrived so quickly that the Thebans were unaware of their approach until they appeared (speed of movement became one of the hallmarks of Alexander's troops). Alexander encamped and bided his time before attacking, but eventually the citadel was assaulted in a series of fierce sallies and the Macedonian troops broke into the inner city. After much savage slaughter Thebes fell, was razed to the ground, its land was apportioned among Alexander's 'allies' in the League of Corinth, and its population enslaved. This disaster shocked the rest of Greece as well as the allies themselves, and many attributed it to divine wrath brought on by the Thebans' support of Persia in the Persian War of the fifth century. There were interesting exceptions to this harsh treatment: priests and priestesses (so that Alexander could claim reverence towards the gods), guest-friends of and local ambassadors for the Macedonian kings (so that Alexander could show that loyalty was rewarded), and the supposed house of the famous poet Pindar (whether the actual house of a poet of the early fifth century really still existed and was identifiable is open to question), and the descendants of Pindar. By this last gesture, Alexander showed his respect for Greek culture and learning. It is pertinent to note that Pindar deserved special treatment also for having written an *encomium* (eulogy) in honour of Alexander's fifth-century ancestor, King Alexander 'the Philhellene'.

The suppression of the Theban revolt had the desired effect. Other cities sent embassies to the king and punished those of their inhabitants who had supported the Theban cause. In reply to the congratulatory embassy from Athens, Alexander demanded the surrender of several prominent citizens (including the orator Demosthenes) as punishment for the city's wrongs at the battle of

Chaironeia and its later attitude towards King Philip and himself. Alexander relented after a second embassy, no doubt less out of kindness to Athens than from a wish to leave a pacified Greece behind him as his thoughts turned towards Asia and the Persian Empire.

DEFEAT OF THE PERSIAN EMPIRE

The Persian Background

Leaving aside for the moment Alexander's original intentions in setting out for Asia, it is necessary to examine briefly the political situation he was to face there. The Persian Empire had been defeated by the combined mainland Greek forces in the Persian Wars of the early fifth century BC, but it was not destroyed. The war had crushed any hopes of Persian domination in Greece proper, but the core of the empire in Asia remained intact. The Great King of Persia, whose capital city was Persepolis, ruled over vast territories, roughly covering modern Turkey, Iran, Iraq, the Middle East, Egypt, and, under looser control, Afghanistan and Pakistan as far as India. The lands were divided into administrative units called satrapies, presided over by provincial governors called satraps. It has already been noted that Greek cities had existed on the west coast of Asia Minor for centuries, and that their wish for freedom was one cause of the Persian War. After the war these cities remained under Persian control.

By virtue of her wealth and political influence, Persia had also played a role in the Peloponnesian War between Athens and Sparta in the last three decades of the fifth century. After that, a peace treaty negotiated between the Great King and the Greek states in 386 BC acknowledged that the Greek cities of Asia belonged to the Great King. Despite this internationally recognised treaty, an emotive cry for the 'liberation of the Greeks of Asia Minor' and ultimate revenge against Persia continued to be heard in fourth-century Greece, fuelled by the rhetoric of some of the most powerful orators of the day. This so-called 'King's Peace' of 386 had not, however, included Macedonia among its signatories. Although we have no way of reconstructing what Philip II's intentions were regarding Persia, it is clear that his battle cry (however cynical) of 'freeing the Greeks' fell on the welcoming ears of his Greek 'allies' in the League of Corinth, despite any private fears the mainland Greeks may have had about their Macedonian overlords. This was the situation inherited and exploited by Alexander.

Both Philip and Alexander may have been swayed in their thinking by the state of the Persian Empire in the second half of the fourth century BC. In the first half of that century, a weak Great King had been shaken by a series of satrapal revolts and by the creation of large, powerful, semi-independent satrapies which threatened centralised royal control. Moreover, the Greek cities of Asia were prone to ongoing squabbles between the aristocratic, propertied class, which tended to be pro-Persian in order to preserve the status quo and their vested interests, and the pro-democratic class, which was hostile to Persia and hoped to prosper when freed from her domination. The internal political struggles within some of these cities are well documented. It would be simplistic to claim that the Persian Empire was 'a plum ripe for the plucking' (if indeed that had been the original intention), but one can understand that both Philip and Alexander may have been encouraged to think that their invasions of Asia would not encounter insuperable resistance.

The Struggle against the Persian Great King Darius

After the destruction of Thebes, Alexander returned to Macedonia and made preparations for his expedition, assembling, we are told, his military commanders and discussing plans with them. (The royal council discussing matters of policy with members of the nobility was the traditional style of Macedonian government.) Diodorus alone says that Antipater and Parmenio (eminent aristocratic generals of Philip II) advised Alexander not to leave the kingdom before marrying and producing an heir. This was wise advice, given the typical struggle over the royal succession in Macedonia – as Alexander himself knew all too well – and, as we know with hindsight, might have eased the chaos which ensued after Alexander's untimely death, but the king brushed such conservative counsel aside. He was eager for action and viewed it a disgrace for the appointed leader of the Greeks in the war and the inheritor of his father's army to sit at home celebrating a marriage and awaiting the birth of a child. This incident, of course, illustrates Alexander's impetuous nature, his impatience with cautious advice, and his unquestioning confidence in military success.

Various sacrifices and festivals were held before the expedition set forth. A traditional sacrifice was made to Olympian Zeus at the Macedonian national sanctuary at Dion in southern Macedonia, in the shadow of the mass of Mount Olympus, traditional home of the gods. (Exciting archaeological excavations have begun at Dion which will increase our understanding of this great sanctuary.) Games in honour of Zeus and the Muses were celebrated as well.

In the spring of 334 BC, Alexander and his army went eastward through Thrace and crossed the Hellespont, the natural boundary between Europe and Asia. The sources disagree about the size of his force: estimates of infantry range from 30,000 to 43,000, and of cavalry from 4,000 to 5,000. Various anecdotes are recorded which explicitly compare Alexander's expedition with the Greek force in the fabled Trojan War (the probable site of Troy is not far from the southern shore of the Hellespont). He is said, among other things, to have sacrificed at the tomb of Protesilaus (the first of the Greek contingent sent to Troy to disembark and be killed), to have honoured the tombs of Trojan War heroes such as Achilles, Ajax and Priam, and to have made dedications and sacrifices at the Temple of Athena in Troy (Ilion) itself. This reverence for Homeric legend runs like a thread throughout the sources. Plutarch relates a charming anecdote that Alexander even slept with a copy of Homer's *Iliad* under his pillow. More tellingly, Alexander himself is said to have been the first Macedonian to have leapt ashore in Asia, hurling his spear into the ground to signify that it was spear-won land.

The Persians sent an advance force north to meet Alexander, and the first major battle between the Persian and Macedonian armies took place in 334 BC near the Granicus river in the Troad, east of Troy. The tactics of this battle, and the ancient descriptions of it, have been endlessly debated, but Alexander managed to defeat the Persians despite having to cross the river and attack enemy troops drawn up in a favourable position on the far bank. The recorded number of Persian dead is impossibly large, and that of Macedonian dead suspiciously small, but we are told that the first twenty-five casualties of Alexander's cavalry were honoured with bronze equestrian statues set up at the sanctuary of Zeus at Dion. Moreover, the works were commissioned from Lysippus of Sicyon, the finest sculptor of his day, whom alone Alexander trusted to depict his own image. The scale of this victory monument is unprecedented in the Greek world, and it must have been intended to rival earlier victory monuments from the Persian and Peloponnesian Wars set up at panhellenic sanctuaries like Delphi. Pointedly, Alexander also sent three hundred sets of captured Persian armour to be displayed on the Athenian acropolis with an inscription recording that it was a dedication from Alexander and the Greeks, except the Spartans (who were not members of the League of Corinth).

Alexander made no attempt to follow up his victory by finding the main Persian army, but proceeded down the western coast of Asia Minor 'liberating' the Greek cities there. This involved expelling the pro-Persian aristocrats and installing democratic governments in their stead. Although it has been claimed that Alexander, by these actions, displayed lofty political ideals, it is more likely that he was securing the gratitude of these anti-Persian democrats and using them as a loyal safeguard after he had moved on. His smooth progress was interrupted by resistance at the Ionian city of Miletus and the Carian city of Halicarnassus (modern Bodrum), both of which had Persian garrisons but were eventually reduced after difficult sieges. He continued along the south coast of Turkey through the inhospitably mountainous region of Lycia, receiving the submission of native cities there. Part of the area could only be traversed along the shoreline, the alternative being treacherous mountain passes. Finally he reached Pisidia and the plain of Pamphylia (in the region of modern Antalya) in 334–3 BC.

At this stage, Alexander made a year-long detour inland through central Turkey to Phrygia, although he faced stiff resistance on the way from the native cities of Pisidia. His military objective is unclear, since the Persian forces were far to the east in Babylon. However, during this period one of the most famous episodes of his expedition took place when he reached the city of Gordion, capital city of Phrygia, not far from modern Ankara.

There was a legend about a poor man called Gordius, who owned a cart with a curious 'knot' connecting it to its yoke. Various portents concerning the yoke were interpreted as a divine manifestation from Zeus. Later, when Gordius's son Midas arrived among the Phrygians in the same cart, they took it as the fulfilment of an oracle which had stated that a cart would bring them a king who would put an end to their civil strife. Midas was declared king, and the cart was dedicated to Zeus on the acropolis of Gordion. (The Great Tumulus excavated at Gordion may well be the tomb of King Midas, who died at the end of the eighth century BC. His skeleton and the impressive grave goods and wooden furniture are currently on display at the Museum of Anatolian Civilisations in Ankara. This historical Midas may lie behind the fabled King Midas, known for his donkey's ears and 'golden touch'.)

A legend more relevant to Alexander said that anyone who untied the knot of the yoke was destined to rule Asia (or, in another account, the whole world). We are told that Alexander was 'seized with a longing' (a precise phrase in Greek which is used several times in Arrian to indicate a deep and not always rational determination on Alexander's part) to go to the acropolis and see the cart and the knot of the yoke.

Two versions exist of what happened. The simple account is that Alexander deduced how to draw out from the cart-pole the pin which held the knot together, and so removed the pole from the yoke. The more swashbuckling story records Alexander drawing his sword and cutting through the knot, which is, of course, the basis of the modern expression 'to cut the Gordian knot' (i.e. to solve a problem quickly and boldly regardless of the intervening difficulties). Whatever the true account, Alexander's entourage felt that the prophecy about the knot had been fulfilled, especially when thunder and lightning that night seemed to be a further sign from heaven. Such divine prophecies of Alexander's predestined success play a large role in all of the ancient sources.

The army then returned south through the region of Cappadocia, and crossed the formidable Taurus Mountains of Cilicia through the pass known as the 'Cilician Gates' (this pass is the only route from north to south through these mountains even today, and the modern highway roughly follows the line of the ancient road). The pass was guarded by Persian troops, who fled at Alexander's approach. The army reached the much more hospitable coastal plain of eastern Cilicia at Tarsus (later to be the birthplace of St Paul), east of modern Mersin, causing the same retreating Persians to flee to the Great King before they had time to sack it.

Alexander experienced his first illness at Tarsus, attributed either to fatigue or to a swim in the icy waters of the Cydnus river. The king was afflicted by cramp and fever so severe that all of his physicians despaired except one, Philip of Acarnania (an area of west-central Greece), who proposed to administer a risky draught of strong drugs. Most sources claim that Alexander had received a letter stating that Philip was intending to poison him. In a dramatic gesture, Alexander handed the letter to the doctor at the moment he drank the potion. The rumour was untrue, and Alexander recovered fully and richly rewarded Philip. Arrian states the moral of the tale: the king demonstrated to his friend that he trusted him, and to his entourage that he did not suspect his friends and was steadfast even when facing death.

The Battle of Issus

After various forays in eastern Cilicia, Alexander learned that the Great King Darius had assembled his army at Sochi in eastern Syria, and he advanced along the coast of the eastern corner of the Mediterranean, following the shore. The plain of Issus in that eastern corner is a narrow coastal strip running north to south in the direction of modern Iskenderun in Turkey (see plate 5) between sea on the west and mountains in the east. The plain was even narrower in antiquity than it is today. After various manoeuvrings for position in which the Macedonians came to be south of the Persians, the two armies met in November 333 in the second major battle of Alexander's expedition. Although the exact location of the battle of Issus on this plain has not been pinpointed, one can immediately see on the ground that this area was not wide enough for the numerically superior Persian force to deploy effectively.

All sources describe in detail the number and type of troops drawn up in their battle formations, and recount the course of the battle. Briefly, after fierce fighting in which Alexander was wounded in the thigh, the king managed to break through the Persian left flank near the mountains, causing the Great King to flee in panic in his chariot. It is probably this moment which is depicted in the famous Alexander Mosaic from Pompeii (now in the

Museo Nazionale, Naples) (see plate 6). Although the Persian cavalry on their right flank had pushed back the Macedonian left in a fierce encounter, when they saw their own left flank collapsing they too joined in headlong flight and the Persian army was routed. The Macedonians pursued the enemy until darkness fell, plundering the royal baggage train in the process, and Alexander captured Darius's chariot and armour, which had been abandoned to increase his speed of flight over difficult terrain. Arrian lists the Persian casualties as 100,000 foot and 10,000 cavalry, including many Persian nobles. Accounts of the Macedonian casualties vary, but no source gives more than 1,200. It is generally agreed by scholars that the number of Persian casualties throughout the campaigns is vastly exaggerated by the sources in an attempt to make the Macedonians seem even more invincible.

The tent and royal family of Darius had also fallen to Alexander. In a famous incident variously recorded, the king entered the tent and was disturbed by the sound of lamentation from the Great King's mother, wife, and children, who believed that Darius was dead. Informed that he was alive, the royal ladies were not violated by Alexander but were treated kindly and confirmed in their royal status and privileges. An additional story describes Alexander and his close friend Hephaistion entering the tent of the queen mother. By mistake the lady made obeisance to Hephaistion instead of the king, since he was the taller. Alexander brushed off the unintended insult, saying gently that Hephaistion too was 'an Alexander'. The ancient sources considered the encounter of Alexander and the royal family a meaningful incident. On the one hand, it illustrated a favourite rhetorical theme of the dramatic 'reversal of fortune' experienced by the royal ladies. On the other hand, Alexander emerges as compassionate, generous in victory, and acting in the way that a good king should act towards a foc against whom he had no personal enmity. A less idealistic interpretation of Alexander's behaviour might be that the queens, who were vitally important in the royal Persian household, were useful hostages in the fight against the Great King.

Darius and some remnants of his army escaped eastward to the Euphrates river, where he reassembled his forces. Alexander visited the

Macedonian wounded at Issus and held a magnificent funeral for the dead in front of the whole army. He proceeded south to Phoenicia and Egypt, receiving the surrender of the cities en route.

Tyre and Egypt

Phoenicia was a strategically important part of the Persian Empire because (along with Cyprus) it supplied the majority of ships for the Great King's navy. During the course of Alexander's progress by land, the allied Persian navy had continued to operate effectively in the Aegean off the coast of Asia Minor. The fear that his army might be cut off from their route home was a continual nagging worry for Alexander, and he took care to put trusted Macedonians in command of the areas he had passed through to ensure that the land route at least was secure.

The Phoenician seaport of Tyre (in modern Lebanon) gave unexpected resistance to Alexander. The pretext for his attack on the fortified island city was the Tyrian refusal to admit the Macedonians for a sacrifice to the 'Tyrian Heracles' (the Phoenician god Melqart). Alexander's reverence for Heracles, from whom his own royal Argead dynasty of Macedonia claimed descent, is marked throughout his career. In truth, Alexander had to subdue Tyre in order to control Phoenicia and guard his lines of communication. The attack on Tyre occupied seven months in 332 BC and is colourfully described in detail by the sources. Military historians consider it a classic example of siege warfare. Alexander constructed a fortified earthen mole connecting the mainland to the island. Land assaults from the mole and the deployment of siege engines were combined with fierce naval attacks (Alexander had by now commandeered part of the Persian fleet) to finally subdue the city. The population was killed or enslaved, and Alexander at last sacrificed to Heracles and staged a magnificent procession in his honour. This episode illustrates not only Alexander's military genius but his unswervable determination to achieve whatever objective he set himself. The two defeats of the Persian army and the capture of Tyre by this point must have inflated his sense of invincibility and taste for military glory.

Although differing in the timing of the embassy

and the details of the proposal, the sources record that envoys arrived from Darius offering Alexander a huge ransom for the return of the royal family, the hand of the Great King's daughter in marriage, all of the lands west of the Euphrates to the 'Greek (Aegean) Sea', and a friendly alliance. Despite advice from the elderly general Parmenio to accept the offer and stop the war, Alexander rudely brushed the envoys aside. (This is the most famous instance of the conflict of opinion played out in council between Alexander and Parmenio. Parmenio said that he would accept the offer if he were Alexander. Alexander countered by saying that he too would accept it, if he were Parmenio.) This brings us to the question of Alexander's intentions at this stage of the expedition. The Greeks of Asia Minor could now be said to have been 'liberated' from Persia in the strict sense of the term, and the offer of all the lands west of the Euphrates would put them in Alexander's hands permanently. Although the original aims of the war of revenge against Persia would therefore seem to have been achieved by this point, Alexander had already campaigned beyond them and clearly intended to continue, as his reply to Darius shows. Although we do not know the scope of Alexander's intentions when he left Macedonia, the alleged pretext for a war of revenge by now had changed explicitly into a larger objective, apparently the defeat and destruction of the Persian Empire.

Alexander entered Egypt after savagely subduing the town of Gaza, the last settlement in the desert between Phoenicia and Egypt. Egypt had been under intermittent Persian control since the last quarter of the sixth century BC, when the Great King Cambyses invaded and conquered the country. It was independent for some sixty years in the fourth century BC, but was reconquered by the Persian Artaxerxes III in 343 BC. The few sources for this period indicate that Persian rule was harsh. As a result, when Alexander arrived in 332 BC he was welcomed by a population prepared to endure another foreign king if this meant the end of Persian domination.

The king paid his respects at the inland pharaonic capital of Memphis (not far from Cairo, and Saqqara with its famous step-pyramid), and sailed north along the Nile to the coast. In the western branch of the Nile delta Alexander founded his greatest city and named it Alexandria after himself. The modern

Egyptian town of the same name lies on top of the ancient city. The sources preserve a charming account of the king 'feeling a strong longing to found a city', appreciating the suitability of the site, and pacing out the line of the walls and the location for various structures within. However this may be, Alexandria has a magnificent setting on the Mediterranean and good natural harbours. Local Greek traders in the region may already have been aware of the potential of a seaport here, and Alexander perhaps just seized upon an opportunity attractively presented to him. Alexandria grew into a great city within a few decades, and became the capital city of the Ptolemaic Empire in Egypt after Alexander's death. By the early third century BC, its proverbial wealth and glittering court life eclipsed other cities of the Greek world, and Alexandria became the undisputed jewel of the Mediterranean. It remained so during Roman times, the vantage-point from which our sources Arrian, Diodorus and Plutarch describe it. Archaeological excavation has always been difficult, since the city has been continuously inhabited since antiquity and because sea-level changes along the coastline have put much of the ancient town under water. Exciting new underwater discoveries in the eastern harbour have recently identified parts of the famous Pharos (lighthouse) of Alexandria, one of the traditional Seven Wonders of the Ancient World, and finds probably from the Ptolemaic Palace area. These major discoveries promise to revolutionise our picture of the ancient city.

The foundation of new cities was a common practice in antiquity as it is in modern times. However, although it appears that both Philip II and Alexander had founded a few cities with their personal names incorporated into the city name (e.g. Philippi, Philippopolis, Alexandropolis), Alexander appears to have been the first person to name a city after himself with the style of nomenclature used for Alexandria (in Greek, 'Alexandreia'). Alexandria in Egypt was his first such city, but he went on to found several other Alexandrias (the exact number is disputed). The phenomenon of Hellenistic city foundations with dynastic names of similar formation (Antiocheia, Seleuceia, Lysimacheia, etc.) is common later, but linguistic historians argue that the first appearance of the place-name 'Alexandreia' would have been a striking departure from normal practice. The closest parallel formation appears to be a city named after a hero who was the son of a god (Chaironeia, named after Chairon). Quite what Alexander intended to signal by this significant change in nomenclature is uncertain. Was he at this stage making some claim to superhuman recognition? He was only twenty-four years old and two years into his expedition.

That such lofty ideas may already have entered Alexander's head is supported by his visit to the Siwah Oasis, in the middle of the desert several days' journey south-west of Alexandria, again as the result of 'a strong longing' to go there. (The sources differ as to whether the visit took place before or after the foundation of Alexandria.) The oasis was the site of the famous Oracle of Ammon, the ram-headed god of the dynastic Egyptians, which was reputed to be particularly accurate in its pronouncements. As early as the fifth century in Greece, this Oracle of Ammon had been identified with the Libyan manifestation of Zeus, king of the Greek gods, who was himself frequently associated with oracles. The sources describe Alexander's journey with considerable relish and maddeningly differing details, and the episode provides important if ambiguous evidence about his divine aspirations.

Some sources say that the army was led across the desert to Siwah by serpents uttering speech; others that two crows acted as guides. Combining all the accounts, it at least seems clear that Alexander entered the inner shrine of the oracle alone, asked the god questions of a secret nature, was satisfied with the equally secret answers, and wrote to his mother Olympias that he would tell her about the visit when he saw her again. Various ancient writers claim that he asked about the murderers of his father, his own paternity (two versions hold that the oracle addressed Alexander as 'son'), and whether or not he was invincible. The truth will never be unravelled, but it seems clear that Alexander's visit to the oracle had a profound and lasting effect on him. He saw himself in a special relationship to Zeus-Ammon throughout his life, apparently believing the god to be his divine father and expecting this to be acknowledged publicly. He regularly sacrificed and prayed to the god, and is said even to have worn the distinctive ram's horns of Ammon (Alexander is shown wearing ram's horns on a coin struck by one of his successors; see plate 7).

The claim to be the son of a god (while acknowledging a human father as well) did not necessarily imply actual divinity for oneself, according to the precedents of Greek mythology. However, historians still endlessly debate whether the assumption of divine attributes such as the horns of Ammon or the lion skin of Heracles (Alexander is depicted in this guise on the so-called 'Alexander Sarcophagus' from Sidon in Phoenicia, now in the Istanbul Archaeological Museum; see plate 8) can be interpreted as anything other than a belief in shared divinity. It is most frustrating that we only know the outward manifestations of Alexander's behaviour, and have no idea what he himself actually thought about it. However, from this evidence it seems safe to suggest that the Alexander in Egypt was a very different man from the Alexander who set forth from Macedonia.

The Battle of Gaugamela and Capture of Royal Persian Cities

In the spring of 331 Alexander's army left Egypt, retraced its steps through Phoenicia, and headed east towards the Euphrates and Tigris rivers in Mesopotamia, the heartland of modern Iraq and Iran. King Darius had meanwhile marshalled a massive army from the eastern areas of the Persian

Empire (unbelievable figures of 1,000,000 infantry, 40,000 cavalry, and 200 scythed chariots are quoted) and was encamped east of the Tigris. There, in the autumn of 331, the third battle between the Macedonian and Persian forces took place at Gaugamela, on artificially levelled ground which provided sufficient room for both armies to deploy. The Persian forces had stood ready in battle formation throughout the previous night and were fatigued when battle commenced. Alexander, we are told, enjoyed an unusually long sleep. To counter the much longer Persian battle-line drawn up before him, Alexander advanced obliquely, leading with his right flank. The Macedonians defused a charge by the scythed chariots by opening ranks to let them pass through; they caused little damage and were subsequently destroyed. As the Persian cavalry moved left to face the advancing Macedonians, a gap appeared in the Persian front line which Alexander stormed through, causing the Persian formation to break and King Darius once again to flee the battlefield. The Macedonian left flank stationed to the rear under the command of Parmenio encountered fierce fighting, but when these Persians realised that their king had fled and that Alexander was wheeling back to assist his left, they too were routed. Again, the estimated numbers of Persian casualties are impossibly high, and those of the Macedonians impossibly low, but after Gaugamela the imperial Persian army never faced battle again.

Alexander ordered a relentless pursuit of the retreating forces even after dark for some thirty-five miles. Although the royal belongings, treasure, chariot and armour were captured at the city of Arbela, Darius escaped and continued his flight into Media, the region south of the Caspian Sea which had been absorbed into the Persian Empire, reckoning correctly that Alexander would first proceed south to the main Persian cities rather than risk his huge force in the inhospitable terrain of Media.

The great cities of the Persian Empire fell quickly to Alexander. In late 331, the ancient city of Babylon surrendered, then Susa where Alexander captured a fabulously rich royal treasury, allegedly including Greek booty brought back to Persia by King Xerxes after his invasion of Greece during the Persian War in 480 BC. In the spring of 330 in a two-pronged attack Alexander reached the capital Persepolis, far to the south-east. Persepolis (in modern Iran) was the residence and burial place of the Great Kings of Persia, and the extensive archaeological remains include palaces, processional ways, grand halls, sculpted reliefs, and fortifications. The Macedonian troops were given free rein to plunder the city.

The Palace of Persepolis was burnt to the ground, a claim which has been corroborated by archaeological excavation. Arrian says that Alexander was advised against this by the cautious Parmenio, on the grounds that the king should not destroy property which was now his, and should not allow the Asians to think that he merely intended to conquer, rather than control, the country. Alexander replied that he wished to exact revenge on the Persians for their sack of Athens in the fifth-century Persian War and for all their other wrongs against the Greeks. The vulgate sources record the romantic story of an Athenian courtesan, Thaïs, who at the end of a drunken victory party raised a torch and urged Alexander to burn the palace so that women in Alexander's entourage might be responsible for destroying the great achievements of the Persians. Whether or not this destruction was premeditated, it is often seen as a loss of control on

1. Head of Alexander from Macedonia, *c.* 300–270 BC (Pella Archaeological Museum inv. no. GL 15. Photo: TAP Service)

2. Alexander the Great, portrait head, third century BC, Greek (marble) (Louvre, Paris, France/Giraudon/Bridgeman Art Library, London)

3. Head of Alexander the Great, after fourth century AD (British Museum, London/Bridgeman Art Library, London)

4. General view of the Sanctuary of Nymphs at Mieza, Macedonia, said to be the school of Aristotle where Alexander studied as a boy (author's photograph)

5. General view of the plain of Issus, the site of Alexander's second battle against the Persian army (author's photograph)

6. The Alexander Mosaic from the House of the Faun, Pompeii, probably depicting Great King Darius fleeing Alexander during the Battle of Issus. Based on a Greek painting of c. 330 BC (Katz Pictures Limited)

7. Silver tetradrachm minted by King Lysimachus of Thrace depicting Alexander wearing
the ram's horns of Zeus Ammon, *c. 297–281 BC* (London, British Museum. Photo:
Hirmer 13.0580V)

8. Detail of Alexander wearing the lion's skin of Herakles on the Alexander Sarcophagus from the royal necropolis of Sidon, Phoenicia, *c*. 320–310 BC (Istanbul, Archaeological Museum 370. Photo: Hirmer 571.2088)

9. Silver tetradrachm of King Ptolemy I of Egypt depicting Alexander wearing an elephant scalp headdress, c. 315–305 BC (Switzerland, Hess/Leu Sale catalogue 15.4.1957, 313. Photo: Hirmer 15.0797V)

10. Hypothetical reconstruction of Alexander's funeral carriage by Stella Miller-Collett. Original 323–321 BC (From Andrew Stewart, *Faces of Power: Alexander's Image and Hellenistic Politics* (University of California Press, 1993), pl. 75. Courtesy of Candace Smith)

11. Gold medallion from Aboukir
in Egypt depicting the idealised
Alexander, *c.* 230–250 AD
(Baltimore, Walters Art Gallery
inv. no. 59.1 Photo: Museum)

12. Idealised head of Alexander
from Dresden. Roman copy based
on a Greek original of *c.* 338–330
BC (Sculpturensammlung ZV–476
(H 174). Photo: Staatliche
Kunstsammlungen Dresden)

Alexander's part. The Macedonians, we are told, rejoiced because they thought the act was carried out by a king with his thoughts on home.

After this, the army moved north in pursuit of King Darius to Ecbatana, the ancient capital of Media near the Caspian Sea. Despite reports that Darius intended to face Alexander's army once more, he again fled eastward and was pursued relentlessly by Alexander beyond the Caspian Sea towards Bactria (the region lying between the Oxus river in the north and the Hindu Kush mountain range in the south). Darius had by now been arrested by some of his high-born officials, including the satrap of Bactria, a man named Bessus. In the late summer of 330, as Alexander was about to overtake the Persians and their royal prisoner, Darius was wounded by his captors, abandoned, and, according to most accounts, died before Alexander reached him. Alexander sent Darius's body to Persepolis and ordered a royal funeral.

With the defeat and death of Darius, Alexander of Macedonia succeeded as Great King of Persia. At Ecbatana before the final pursuit of Darius, he had signalled that the war of revenge by the Greeks against Persia was soon to be over: he disbanded his Thessalian and allied Greek troops, sending them home with vast amounts of booty, and employing those who wished to stay as mercenaries. The Persian Empire had been defeated and effectively destroyed.

THREE

THE FRONTIER
BEYOND

This is a decisive moment in Alexander's career. The war of revenge against Persia was now over, and his allied Greek troops had been sent home. He had conquered vast areas of Asia Minor, the Middle East, Egypt, Iraq and Iran, and had effectively destroyed the Persian Empire, while capturing the enormously wealthy treasuries in the royal capitals. He had assumed the titles and position of Great King, and secured the administration of the empire by the appointment of new Macedonian and Persian satraps as he went along. Although the outlying satrapies of the Persian Empire, roughly comprising modern Afghanistan and Pakistan (this satrapy of 'India' had been loosely held by the Persians), had not at this stage been conquered by him, the nomadic, tribal nature of the north-eastern satrapies probably meant that a concerted revolt against him could not have been sustained for long without the support of the Persian heartland, especially if Macedonian garrisons were left in strategic areas (this is in fact what Alexander did later). Yet Alexander continued to campaign for six more years. It appears that he initially set out on mopping-up operations to quell any revolt after Darius's death. Did he then intend, despite the almost unimaginable geographical and climatic obstacles he would face, to achieve the complete defeat of all Persian territory in person? Even if this was the case, why did he want to go on after that? What was his final objective? When did he decide on his final objective? The answers to these difficult questions can only be attempted, since the sources record little evidence of Alexander's intentions. If indeed he knew the answers himself, he apparently kept his own counsel.

The Pursuit of Bessus

The mopping-up operations consisted of moving east from the Caspian Sea into the region known as Hyrcania in pursuit of the Greek mercenaries in Darius's employ who had escaped after Gaugamela, and of subduing the native peoples in the territories he passed through. Alexander received the surrender of many of the mercenaries, who thereupon joined his own forces. Far more serious was the revolt of the Bactrian satrap Bessus. News came that Bessus had declared himself Great King under the regnal name of Artaxerxes and was gathering a force of Persians, Bactrians, and Scythian allies to face Alexander. The Macedonians continued to pursue him eastward until his final surrender in summer 329 BC.

It is during this period that the sources record various anecdotes and episodes which indicate a change in Alexander's personality. He is said to have assumed Persian dress and the upright tiara of the Great Kings, employing Persian standard-bearers at court and harnessing his horses in Persian style. Plutarch says his dress was modified to look only half-Persian, and that he appeared in this guise first before Persians and his close friends, and only later before the populace as a whole. It is made clear, however, that the Macedonians, even in the beginning, did not approve of these Persian customs and excessive luxury.

Diodorus records that Alexander, like Darius,

accumulated an imperial harem of several hundred women. Many scholars have discounted this merely on the grounds that such behaviour would not have been 'fitting' in a Macedonian king, but this is a subjective view based on modern idolisation of Alexander. It is also at about this time that Alexander is said to have received a visit from the queen of the Amazons, a legendary race of female warriors well known in Greek mythology and, by convention, traditionally resident in remote areas south of the Black Sea. The queen allegedly wished Alexander to father her child, and stayed with him for thirteen days. This connection of Amazons and Alexander the Great most probably arose in the decades or centuries after his death, when the body of tales about Alexander, which Arrian refers to, was growing and being elaborated into his personal mythology, elements of which have penetrated our historical sources. (Recent news reports have announced the find of ancient graves of female warriors in south Russia. Further research may suggest that such people were the historical antecedents of the mythical Amazons.)

Far more disturbing for our picture of Alexander is his behaviour towards two of his trusted

Macedonian friends, the old general Parmenio and his son Philotas. One source says that Philotas's unreliability had been reported to Alexander back in Egypt; at the time the king could not bring himself to think badly of Philotas because of his family connections and did nothing. But now, a threat to Alexander's life arose when a member of his bodyguard developed a grudge against the king and fomented a plot against him. Philotas was told of the conspiracy but did not warn the king, either because he himself was a party to the treason or simply because he was slow to act, perhaps not taking the threat seriously. The conspiracy was at last revealed to Alexander. Philotas was arrested and accused before the assembled Macedonians of concealing his knowledge of the plot from Alexander. He was convicted and immediately killed along with other accused individuals. Another man, Alexander of Lyncestis (a region of Macedonia), was also executed on a three-year-old charge of treason. We may note that members of this man's family had already been killed earlier in the struggles surrounding Alexander's accession to the Macedonian throne.

Alexander's suspicions then turned in the direction of Parmenio, left behind at Ecbatana in charge of the royal treasury. It is said that the king may have believed that the father must have been implicated in his son's crime, and therefore was also guilty. Or, even if Parmenio was innocent in this regard, Alexander may have envied Parmenio's popularity with the troops and feared their swing to him when he learned of his son's death. Alexander despatched orders for the death of Parmenio, to be carried on racing camels which would arrive before the news of the execution of Philotas. The reaction of the troops to the death of Parmenio, the loyal general of King Philip II, verged on mutiny. Diodorus says, significantly, that Alexander gathered into a 'Disciplinary Company' all those who were angered by the murder as well as those who wrote home any remarks not complimentary to the king (this implies that a strict form of censorship and espionage was in practice). Kept isolated, these trouble-makers could not infect the rest of the army.

What are we to make of these events? From the start Alexander seems to have been attracted to the perquisites of the role of Great King, and to have alienated his fellow Macedonians who had defeated the 'barbarian' Persians whom he now emulated. His ruthless reaction to suspicions of treason may indicate paranoiac tendencies about the supposed enemies within (once trusted friends), now that the enemies from without had largely been defeated. He seems to have been moving towards a future marked by increasing intolerance of dissent and consequent cruel punishment, regardless of the effect it might have.

In the spring of 329 BC, Alexander pursued Bessus into Bactria by the incredible achievement of crossing the Hindu Kush mountain range (the ancient Caucasus Mountains). We are told that he founded various cities called Alexandria en route. Given that some archaeological investigations in Afghanistan were in their preliminary stages when disrupted years ago by the continuing civil war there, the identification of most of these sites on the ground is uncertain, as indeed is their ultimate fate. All sources record a similar blend of population: natives, camp followers, and volunteers from the mercenaries. This is a very mixed composition of peoples with no inherent relationship with each other. It is probably correct to see these settlements not as 'cities' in the full urban sense, but as fortified outposts intended to signify a military presence and pacify the surrounding area.

Bessus proceeded north and ravaged the countryside to hamper Alexander's pursuit. One of the miracles of Alexander's expedition throughout was the success of the army in securing provisions for several thousand troops and camp followers even in inhospitable terrain, which must have been a nightmarish and never-ending task for his quartermasters, requiring excellent native scouts. Arrian says that the army none the less continued to advance through thick snow, with great difficulty and lacking necessities, but was not stopped. Bessus retreated north across the Oxus river (the northern boundary of Afghanistan) into the region called Sogdiana. After subduing the main cities of Bactria and putting the region under satrapal control, Alexander, before his next major step into the unknown, disbanded the oldest Macedonian troops who were no longer fit for service and sent them home along with the Thessalian volunteers who had remained with him. In pursuit of Bessus, it took Alexander's remaining troops five days to cross the mighty Oxus river on rafts made from animal hides stuffed with chaff.

By now Bessus had been betrayed and arrested by his allies, and was handed over to the king, bound, naked, and wearing a wooden collar. He was accused of the regicide of King Darius and whipped. This was the pretext of Bessus's punishment, but clearly his revolt against Alexander was the real cause of his savage treatment. One tradition says that his nose and ears were cut off, and that he was sent back to the family of Darius, who humiliated and abused him before finally cutting his body into small pieces and scattering them. Plutarch records an even more grisly fate. While alive Bessus was tied to two trees bent inwards towards each other, and was torn apart when the trees were released.

Alexander the Great had made clear how a revolt against him would be treated.

The North-eastern Satrapies and the Death of Cleitus

Alexander spent the summer of 329 in Sogdiana, advancing not without resistance to Maracanda (Samarkand) and then the River Tanais, or Jaxartes (the ancients used the names interchangeably; the modern name is the Syr-Darya). Here on the river Alexander founded a city called Alexandria Eschate ('the Furthest'), a settlement in the extreme north-east of his empire even as the Egyptian Alexandria was in the extreme south-west. We are told that, again, Alexander appreciated the suitability of the site, seeing it as a base for an invasion of Scythia to the north and as a fortified defence against local barbarian raids. A city wall was constructed, and he settled there a mix of Greek mercenaries, local volunteers, and time-expired Macedonian veterans. The cities of Sogdiana were brutally captured and their populations murdered or enslaved. Alexander crossed the Tanais, again with hide rafts, in pursuit of the Scythians but turned back at the news of successful actions by Spitamenes, a Sogdian nobleman and former ally of Bessus, who had attacked the Macedonian garrison at Samarkand and a column sent to relieve them. Spitamenes fled, but Alexander ravaged the country in revenge before wintering in Bactria at Zariaspa (today Balkh) south of the Oxus.

Early in the spring of 328, Alexander recrossed the Oxus back into Sogdiana, harshly suppressing any signs of revolt and settling cities in the direction of Scythia, where Spitamenes had now fled as a base from which to launch attacks on Bactria and Sogdiana. Towards the end of that campaigning year the various Macedonian forces converged on Samarkand, where a religious festival and sacrifice were being celebrated. A famous episode occurred during the ensuing banquet when the participants were well into their cups.

In the course of the drunken conversation, it was claimed that Alexander's achievements had surpassed not only those of certain gods and heroes but also the deeds of his father Philip. Cleitus, a Macedonian whose sister was Alexander's childhood nurse and who had saved the king's life at the Battle of the Granicus river, became enraged at such grotesque flattery. Long disaffected by the king's adoption of Persian ways, in the heat of his drunkenness Cleitus launched a ferocious tirade against Alexander. The others restrained the king, who in fury moved to strike him, but after further insults, Alexander struck and killed Cleitus. The king was devastated by remorse; some accounts say that he immediately tried to kill himself, others that he retired to his bed for days in inconsolable grief.

How are we to interpret this incident? Arrian exculpates Alexander by blaming the rashness of Cleitus, pitying the king's weakness in the face of drunkenness and anger, and praising him for the immediate recognition that he had done a grievous wrong. It is clear, however, that Alexander experienced a catastrophic loss of control which led to the murder of a friend from his boyhood to whom he owed his life. Drunkenness may explain the deed, but, even with his subsequent remorse, it can hardly excuse it. It is significant that the dispute arose in the first place when Alexander reacted to an insult to himself and his own greatness, and could not tolerate it.

The campaign went on regardless. After fierce encounters against various divisions of Alexander's army, Spitamenes was betrayed by his Scythian allies and his head was sent to Alexander. The troops wintered at Nautaca, a town somewhere south of the Oxus.

The Passage to India

In the spring of 327, Alexander journeyed south across the Hindu Kush, capturing en route two 'rocks' (fiercely defended mountain-top fortresses), and returned south to Bactria. Four episodes occur during this period which are important for our interpretation of Alexander's career. Firstly, prisoners taken at the capture of the Rock of Sogdiana included the Bactrian nobleman Oxyartes and his family. One of his daughters was a girl of exceptional beauty named Rhoxane. It is said that Alexander fell in love with her, and married her instead of just keeping her as his war-captive. We do not know if his intentions were primarily personal or partly political, but the king evidently did not think that a Bactrian woman was beneath his status. This marriage may have pleased Alexander's native subjects, but one wonders how the Macedonian rank and file felt about a barbarian queen. The next generation of Macedonian kings, if descended from this marriage, would be half-barbarian.

The second episode is Alexander's attempt to initiate at court the ceremony of proskynesis, a traditional act of homage performed by Persian subjects before their Great King. Both the exact nature of the act itself (which appears to range from a bow and a blown kiss to complete prostration, depending upon the rank of the subject) and the conflated sequence of events concerning its introduction have been endlessly debated. The important point is that the Greeks considered such abasement of one human being to another abjectly servile. Two incidents stand out. A loving cup was passed at a dinner party; those who drank from it made appropriate obeisance to Alexander, and received a kiss from the king. A notable refusal was made by Callisthenes of Olynthus, the official historian accompanying the campaign. When Alexander then declined to kiss him, Callisthenes replied with the well-known retort, 'So I go off a kiss the less'. Also in this context rhetorical speeches are recorded before assembled Macedonians and Persians concerning the boundaries between human and divine honours, with the proposal that Alexander was now worthy of the latter because of his exploits. The same Callisthenes voiced robust opposition to this view. When one of Alexander's friends laughed at a Persian who then offered proskynesis, the idea of including Macedonians in the ceremony was dropped.

Was Alexander as Great King merely trying to spread a traditional Persian court ceremony (which his Persian subjects performed as a matter of course) to all of his subjects, regardless of their ethnic origin, or did he now have some deeper notion that he had transcended mortal limits and deserved divine honours? We cannot know the answer, although the proskynesis episode is often used as evidence for Alexander's wish for deification, but it is clear that the Macedonians were uneasy that their king had transgressed the bounds of propriety regarding honours and had tried to lower them to the same level as his Persian subjects.

Callisthenes was also connected with the third significant episode, the so-called 'Royal Pages' Conspiracy' against the king. Hermolaos, one of the royal pages said to be a pupil of Callisthenes, had been humiliated in public by Alexander after a hunting incident. The outrage rankled and spread, and a group of the boys conspired to kill the king. When the plot was revealed to Alexander, the boys were arrested and under torture confessed to their crime, implicating other conspirators. The boys alleged that Callisthenes had put them up to the plot, and Alexander readily believed the worst about Callisthenes because he had already come to hate him (no doubt because of the insults detailed above) and because Callisthenes was close to Hermolaos. Callisthenes was consequently arrested. Two versions of his fate exist: he was either tortured and hanged without delay, or kept a captive in chains until he died of disease.

The death of Callisthenes has two important consequences for the history of Alexander. Firstly, his 'official history' of the campaigns could not have included any material after 328, and no information from him is therefore transmitted by our secondary sources after this point. Secondly, the cause of Callisthenes was taken up by later writers because of his relationship with Aristotle, and, supposedly, the Peripatetic School of philosophy. In these quarters Alexander was virulently attacked for his treatment of Callisthenes, and this unflattering picture of the king can be seen in certain later histories.

Finally, it was probably just before leaving Bactria for India in 327 that Alexander enrolled native cavalry to swell his depleted numbers of Macedonians, and ordered 30,000 youths from the Upper Satrapies to be taught Greek and trained in the Macedonian art of war. They were given the emotive name 'Epigoni' (the 'Descendants' or 'Posterity'). Now the proud and invincible Macedonian army was to be diluted by barbarians, and they took the change badly.

The Advance to the Indus River

In the campaigning season of 327 Alexander came south across the Hindu Kush, probably via the Kushan Pass, and, leaving a sizeable garrison in Bactria, he proceeded east towards India via the Kabul river valley (the term 'India' is used here throughout in the ancient sense to denote the geographical regions of Pakistan and the modern state of India). This vast area had been nominally under Persian control, but was in practice ruled by native princes who were frequently at war with each other. We do not know when Alexander decided on this campaign, or whether it was a natural extension of his apparent plan to conquer all former Persian territory in person, thereby holding all of 'Asia' (as it was then conceived), or whether at some point he had seen a further horizon beyond his victories in the Upper Satrapies. An advance force was sent ahead to prepare for the crossing of the Indus. Throughout the winter of 327/6 the main force under Alexander attacked and subdued cities as they advanced through Swat, often after fierce and prolonged fighting. Many cities were destroyed and their inhabitants captured or massacred.

A major obstacle was the so-called 'Rock of Aornus', just to the west of the Indus, a virtually impregnable mountain stronghold to which natives from various cities had fled to escape Alexander. There was a legend that even the hero Heracles, son of Zeus, had not been able to capture the Rock, which made Alexander all the more determined to do so. His emulation of Heracles, mythical ancestor of the Macedonian royal house, is evident throughout his life, as is his striving to outdo the feats of the hero. First securing and fortifying the cities around the Rock, Alexander besieged Aornus. The army occupied a favourable vantage-point apparently pointed out by natives who had already surrendered. When, with considerable effort, a siege mound was constructed on which catapults and siege engines could be deployed against the Rock, the natives offered to surrender, hoping to abandon their position under cover of darkness. Alexander and his men scaled the Rock when the withdrawal had begun, turning back and killing many of the retreating barbarians. Aornus was captured and garrisoned.

Another Greek god who featured large in Alexander's Indian campaign was Dionysus. It has already been mentioned that Dionysus was widely worshipped in Macedonia, as indeed elsewhere, and that Alexander's mother was an enthusiastic devotee. According to legend, Dionysus and his army had invaded and conquered India, and scenes of his triumphal return to the west are frequently depicted in scenes from ancient art. Arrian records how Alexander's army saw traces of Dionysus's presence in India: a city called Nysa (the name of the god's nurse), one called Meros ('Thigh': Dionysus was born from the thigh of Zeus), and ivy (a plant traditionally associated with the god). Comparisons between the two Indian campaigns, and between Dionysus and Alexander, became inevitable and were certainly current before Arrian's day.

In the spring of 326 Alexander's army crossed the Indus on boats and over the floating bridge which had been built by his advance force. He had already received from its Indian ruler Taxiles the surrender of Taxila, the greatest city between the Indus and the Hydaspes, its first tributary to the east (Taxila is now a remarkable archaeological site to the north-west of modern Islamabad). Alexander was welcomed upon his arrival there, was generous to the surrounding Indians, and departed for the east leaving a Macedonian satrap and garrison in the city.

An appreciation of the geography of this area is vital to the understanding of Alexander's progress. The Indus is a complex river system, and extends to the east through the Punjab. It is joined by four major tributaries: from west to east, the Hydaspes (the modern Jhelum river), the Acesines (now the Chenab river), the Hydraotes (the Ravi river, on which the modern city Lahore is situated), and the Hyphasis (the Beas or Sutlej river). The Ganges river system lies across the plain further east.

The Battle against Porus

One native prince who refused to submit to Alexander was Porus, who ruled the land between the Hydaspes and Acesines rivers. The Macedonians advanced to the Hydaspes to face his massive army assembled on the east bank of the river. He is said to have had 30,000 infantry, 4,000 horse, 300 chariots, and 200 elephants. Western armies had never faced elephants on the field of battle before Alexander's invasion of India. Some of the Indian rulers whom Alexander had already subdued had possessed elephants. Alexander, who was immediately able to appreciate a military innovation and tactical advantage, took pains to capture these beasts and add them to his own forces, but he had not yet faced elephants in battle. Porus's two hundred elephants were a formidable force by any standards. The threat they posed in terms of strength and unstoppable forward movement was made more serious by the fact that cavalry horses unused to the animals refused to go near them out of fear.

The battle against Porus at the Hydaspes was arguably the fiercest pitched battle ever fought by Alexander. He had to force the crossing of a major river which was heavily defended against him, and then engage a superior force including elephants, which could by their presence neutralise his previously invincible cavalry. The king sent back to the Indus for his boats to be dismantled and carried to join him.

Alexander's initial strategy consisted of an elaborate series of deceptions over several days. A rumour was spread that he would not cross until the depth of the river fell, and he feigned several night crossings both up- and downstream from his camp.

When Alexander felt confident that Porus was confused about his intentions and had relaxed his vigilance, he made his move. Leaving a sizeable presence in his base camp under the command of Craterus, Alexander moved his main force to a crossing place some seventeen miles upstream under cover of a dark and stormy night. A secondary force was to cross a short way downstream from this when Alexander was clear. Although Alexander's men initially reached a large island in the middle of the river rather than the bank opposite, they finally struggled ashore and joined up with their comrades. Moving south to Porus's main camp, they defeated an advance force under the command of Porus's son.

Porus drew up his army at right angles to the river, stationing his infantry and elephants in the centre and his cavalry on both flanks. In order to keep the Indian cavalry (who were used to elephants) away from the main infantry engagement, Alexander mounted a cavalry attack with his right, causing Porus to send the cavalry on his own right flank around to support those under pressure on his left. A detachment of Macedonian cavalry from Alexander's left encircled the Indian forces from behind and attacked their cavalry in the rear as Alexander attacked them from the front. The infantry forces then engaged in the centre. The Macedonian infantry proved superior, as the Indian line was disrupted by their fleeing cavalry and by wounded elephants which went berserk and trampled Indians and Macedonians alike. Porus was utterly defeated, and the rout increased when Craterus's forces crossed the river from the base camp and joined the fray. All of the elephants were either killed or captured. The importance which Alexander placed upon elephants as a new-found instrument of war is manifested by his depiction in a headdress fashioned from an elephant skin (see plate 9).

When Porus was brought into Alexander's presence, he was asked what he wished to be done with him. He replied that he wished to be treated like a king, and Alexander complied with his request, confirming him as king in his territory and increasing his domain. This incident is related by the sources to show Alexander generous in victory, but from it we see that Alexander intended to rule vast areas of India through native client-kings who owed loyalty to him alone. On the Hydaspes, Alexander founded the city of Nicaea ('Victory') in memory of his defeat of Porus, and a city named Bucephala, after his boyhood horse Bucephalas, which had recently died aged about thirty years.

The Mutiny on the Hyphasis River

Alexander continued his progress eastward through the Punjab through the intense heat of the late spring and mid-summer of 326 and the approach of the monsoon season, receiving the surrender of native cities and princes, and defeating any pockets of resistance (only a few held him up for long). The roaring Acesines river was crossed with difficulty and the loss of several boats; the Hydraotes posed no problem. He advanced to the fourth tributary of the Indus river, the Hyphasis, the most south-eastern of these rivers. The sources record that Alexander had heard favourable reports of the area beyond the Hyphasis: that the land was fertile, the population orderly, and the elephants plentiful. He was eager to proceed across this river and continue the war so long as there were enemies remaining.

The Macedonian troops, however, had suffered enough, and refused to go further. Although the

alleged reason is that they could no longer bear to
see Alexander continually running risks, it is easy to
imagine the state of mind of men who had endured
constant danger, fear, hardship, deprivation,
warfare, wounds and disease for some eight years,
and who were now many thousands of miles from
home, without any apparent end to their campaign.
Dissent spread throughout the camp, and Alexander
is reported to have urged them on to further
endeavours with a rousing speech. (Diodorus states
that he first allowed the men to plunder the
surrounding countryside in an effort to cheer them
up.) A long speech by Alexander, and a reply by one
of his men, is recorded in Arrian. Whether or not
this speech contains the germ of what was actually
said, or is a fictitious elaboration by Arrian, is
unknown and disputed. In it Alexander anticipates
the conquest of the whole known world, as he
understood it (geographical knowledge in antiquity
was not always accurate). If these sentiments are
indeed genuine, Alexander's horizon once again
appears to have shifted to a further goal beyond
what he had conceived in Bactria.

The troops could not be persuaded to change
their minds even when the king threatened to

dismiss those who wished to return home and to carry on alone with volunteers. Alexander then sulked in his tent for three days, not even speaking to his closest friends. Finally, the king realised that he had lost, and announced to his generals that he had decided to turn back. The news was received with joy by the troops. The great campaign had reached its most eastern limit, but the army had a long way to go before seeing Macedonia again, and many of them never did.

FOUR

RETURN AND DEATH

The Departure from India

In the end, Alexander's schemes of further conquest were defeated by his army's refusal to go further, and he was forced to retreat and return to the west. The army retraced its steps back across the tributaries of the Indus to the Hydaspes, where a fleet of transport ships had been readied. The return journey took the troops south down the Indus to the sea. Arrian recounts the details of the trip in his *Indika*, based on the account of Nearchus, the admiral of the fleet. The flotilla suffered considerable damage in the fierce currents of the river. A sizeable force accompanied it by land along the banks of the Indus, receiving the submission of the local peoples or subduing them by force.

A particularly fierce campaign was waged in

326/5 BC against the Mallian people, a self-governing Indian tribe living on the east bank of the Indus between the Hydraotes and Hydaspes rivers. Numerous cities of the Malli were captured with great savagery, until their remaining combined forces, numbering some 50,000, converged upon a strongly defended city. Alexander encircled the city and mounted a siege against it. When the Macedonians had penetrated the city as far as the citadel, they mounted an attack scaling the walls by means of ladders. Alexander, leading from the front as always, mounted the wall but was isolated upon it in full view of the enemy when the ladder beneath him broke. Here occurred one of the most foolhardy acts of Alexander's career. So that he would not be such a visible target, the king leapt from the wall down into the city and engaged in hand-to-hand combat with the Indians within. A few Macedonians managed to come to his aid, but Alexander received a severe chest wound and finally became unconscious from loss of blood. The sources paint a vivid picture, with many variations, of his comrades fighting while standing over his body, one allegedly protecting him with the sacred shield from the Temple of Athena at Ilion (Troy).

In the end the attacking Macedonians broke through the wall of the citadel, and massacred every inhabitant they could find, including women and children. Alexander's unconscious body was retrieved and carried off to safety on his shield. This was not the first time that Alexander had been wounded during the course of the campaigns, but he somehow managed to survive this wound, which was by far the most serious he had received. Rumours of the king's death circulated the camp, which caused great lamentation, but in due course he was reunited with the main body of troops. Their joy was unbounded when they saw their king get up from a litter, walk, and mount his horse. Arrian records that Alexander was angry when some of his friends blamed him for taking risks, because he knew it to be true. The Malli surrendered unconditionally, and a Macedonian was appointed satrap over them. This campaign marked a new level in the savagery displayed by Alexander and his troops.

Throughout the remainder of 325 BC, the army proceeded south along the Indus river. Some of the forces travelled by ship, and others marched along the banks. More new cities and ship-stations were fortified, and Alexander received the surrender of several more Indian kings. Finally they reached Patala in the Indus delta, fortifying its citadel and constructing shipyards and docks to make it into a permanent port. The journey through this complex delta was not all smooth: on occasions the ships were damaged by storms, stranded by tides, and the captains were totally reliant on native pilots. Time was spent exploring the various mouths of the delta to find the most navigable branches for the fleet.

Alexander planned to send his fleet back west along the coast and up into the Persian Gulf to the mouths of the Tigris and Euphrates rivers. Some troops were sent back along a northern route through Afghanistan, but Alexander himself led a large detachment of troops overland in order to dig wells and stockpile provisions for the fleet as they put into land. They advanced through the Makran, ancient Gedrosia, attacking the Oritai and Gedrosian peoples and receiving their surrender as they went on.

The sixty-day march through this Gedrosian desert nearly spelled disaster for the expedition. The terrain is inhospitable in the extreme. The sources present a vivid picture of the suffering of the troops, who had little food and hardly any water. In order to stay alive they were forced to take a more inland route and send supplies to the coast for the fleet. The troops were reduced to pilfering sealed rations destined for the coast. It is reported that they feared imminent death from starvation more than punishment from their king. They endured unbearable heat and ceaseless thirst, and killed and ate their pack animals, pretending that the beasts had already died or had collapsed from fatigue. Many men were left behind to die since the wheeled vehicles could not traverse the terrain and had, in any case, few animals left to draw them. A disastrous flash flood in a dry gulley killed most of the women and children and the surviving animals. Alexander reputedly underwent the same torments as his men and was seen to pour on to the ground a helmet full of water since not all of his men could drink from it.

Many have argued that this ill-fated journey across the desert was one of Alexander's few major tactical mistakes, although others hold that the conditions were not really as dire as the sources paint them. The opinions of the ancient writers on Alexander's motives are intriguing. Nearchus the admiral alone claimed that Alexander decided on this route through ignorance of its difficulty, but most writers claim that Alexander had heard that this desert had been crossed with an army only by Cyrus the Great (the founder of the Persian Empire) and the Assyrian Queen Semiramis, and that he aspired to emulate the achievements of these legendary figures. I would argue that either ignorance of conditions or a romantic whim points to a serious lapse of judgement. In any event, Alexander was lucky that some of his troops survived.

The army rested at the end of their desert crossing, and went on through the region of Carmania (between Gedrosia and Iran). Most sources record a celebratory revel of colossal scale, with musical and athletic events witnessed by drunken troops drawn along on carts adorned as Dionysiac bowers. Arrian states clearly that he does not believe such reports, but the comparisons between Alexander's expedition to India and that of Dionysus have already been noted. Nor should we underestimate the relief expressed by men who had nearly died in the desert and who were given the chance to celebrate freely after months of deprivation.

Alexander and his troops returned to the heartland of Persia during 324. This journey is described briefly in the sources, but it is marked by Alexander's harsh punishment of both Macedonian and Persian satraps who were accused of disobedience or corruption as he passed through. Many no doubt had never expected Alexander to return, and had taken upon themselves extreme powers amounting to royal prerogatives. Alexander could not tolerate this, and executed several officials in what has been likened to a 'reign of terror' (the phrase used by the eminent historian Ernst Badian). Regardless of what these actions reveal about Alexander's increasingly autocratic behaviour and deteriorating temperament, they clearly demonstrate the fragility of the administrative arrangements he had put into place on his outward journey.

Alexander reached the royal Persian city of Pasargadae, where he was enraged to see the defilement of the tomb of Cyrus the Great. He appointed Aristoboulos, one of Arrian's two main historical sources, as overseer of its restoration. This is a further indication of the regard in which he held King Cyrus, who was exempt from the stigma of the later Persian Wars in Greece. He returned to Persepolis, which his troops had already looted and burnt, hanging the acting satrap and punishing others on his way.

In 324 BC they reached the royal city of Susa, and here Alexander staged a mass wedding of his highest-ranking officers to native ladies of noble birth. Alexander (who was already married to the Bactrian Rhoxane) also married Statira, the eldest daughter of Darius, and another Persian lady as well. We are told specifically that the ceremonies were in the Persian style. In addition, some 10,000 Macedonians who had already 'married' Asian women registered them and were given generous wedding gifts. It would appear that Alexander was urging a policy of racial fusion between Persians and Macedonians and the creation of a mixed-race ruling class to govern his empire. It is noteworthy that after Alexander's death we only hear of one of the noblewomen still married to a Macedonian general. This was Apama, daughter of the Sogdian Spitamenes, who married a general named Seleucus and became his queen when he declared himself king of the Syrian (Seleucid) Empire. Alexander continued his beneficence by discharging the debts of all his soldiers and by presenting honours and decorations to officers and men distinguished for their bravery and deeds. At this point the 30,000 Epigoni from the Upper Satrapies joined Alexander, dressed in Macedonian fashion and trained in the Macedonian art of war.

The Macedonian rank and file disapproved very much of Alexander's policy of fusion between Macedonians and Persians. It is recorded that even the bridegrooms did not like the Persian-style weddings, and that no one liked to see Alexander in Persian dress or promoting those who espoused Persian customs. They thought that the arrival of the Epigoni and the incorporation of native units into the infantry and cavalry signalled the end of his reliance upon the Macedonian troops who had endured so many adventures and hardships with their king.

These grievances exploded into mutiny again at the city of Opis on the Tigris, after Alexander had explored the delta of the Tigris which flows into the Persian Gulf. When the king proposed to discharge the time-expired and unfit veterans and send them home, keeping only those who wished to stay, the troops interpreted this as an insult to them and reacted in fury. The ringleaders said that they would all go home and leave him to fight along with his father – by whom they meant Ammon. Alexander was incandescent with rage, had the ringleaders arrested, and delivered a long speech justifying his career and the campaign (much of the preserved speech in Arrian is probably his own rhetorical elaboration of what he thought Alexander said). Again the king withdrew to his tent for three days, but, when he began to install Persians in military commands, the Macedonians flocked to his tent and begged forgiveness. At a banquet of reconciliation, Alexander proclaimed both Persians and Macedonians as his kinsmen.

Alexander's special friend Hephaistion died at Ecbatana in 324 BC, after an illness lasting a week. Alexander was prostrate with grief, and the sources vie with each other in detailing the extravagant things he did in his despair (ordering the manes and tails of all the cavalry animals to be shorn in mourning, to give but one example). Diodorus describes in detail the elaborate funeral monument he planned for Hephaistion in Babylon, and Alexander sent to the oracle at Ammon enquiring what honours it would be appropriate to pay his friend. Yet the king was not to survive Hephaistion for long. The army proceeded to Babylon, and he entered the city in 323 BC despite dire warnings from seers, and several other portents that danger would befall him there.

The account of Alexander's last days are derived in part from a source called the 'Royal Journals' by Arrian and Plutarch. The form and content of these journals have been widely debated without universal agreement, since they do not seem to be official documents such as might have been compiled by Alexander's secretariat, but an account mainly of the excesses of Alexander's last days on earth. They are generally regarded as a bogus document forged at some stage for some reason by some unknown person to cast a gloss on the events of that turbulent period, but there is no consensus of scholarly opinion beyond that. However we are to interpret these journals, they record serious drinking sessions between Alexander and a man called Medius, after which the king contracted a fever. The fever did not abate even though Alexander rested and was carried several times to bathe in the river, offering sacrifices each time. For days he ate little, became extremely ill, and finally was unable to talk although he could still recognize his officers. We are told that the army insisted on filing past his bed, and his last actions were to greet each one by raising his head and making a sign with his eyes. He died shortly afterwards.

Many have tried to make posthumous diagnoses of Alexander's illness, but we will never know for certain what it was. Clearly the years of hardship and the various wounds he sustained took their toll and probably made his system less able to resist the fever. Perhaps the final drinking bouts exacerbated his condition. Poison was of course alleged, and the sources tell us various stories about possible motives and culprits, but, on the whole, dismiss these tales as malicious rumours. In the end, Alexander was only a mortal like all men.

It adds to the mystery of Alexander the Great that so much uncertainty still surrounds his last days and death, but with his passing the dream was shattered, and it was left to lesser men to pick up the pieces.

FIVE

ALEXANDER'S PERSONALITY

I do not believe that it is possible to attempt a reconstruction of Alexander's personality without attributing to him motives which are not found in the ancient sources — our best, but ultimately unsatisfactory, evidence about him. I have therefore tried in the previous chapters to stay close to our sources, although it is a problem that the recorded opinions of Arrian, Diodorus and Plutarch (all of whom lived hundreds of years after Alexander) on the king's behaviour may not be preferable to those of any modern scholar who thinks that he understands Alexander and what motivated him to act as he did in any given instance. The historiography of Alexander the Great (by which I mean the study of the histories written about him) is in itself a fascinating overview of trends in historical writing and the personalities of their authors. I hope that I have not 'identified' myself with Alexander and written an account based on what would have led me to act as he did, but perhaps this is what all biographers do despite their protestations to the contrary. What follows is not a full assessment of the man, but a short discussion of aspects of his character which I think are illuminated in the sources.

There is no doubt that Alexander was a brilliant military tactician. His battle plans are still studied in military colleges in Europe and America. Elements of his genius were speed of movement, an appreciation of terrain, the use of his troops in the most advantageous way, and a charismatic and inspiring quality of leadership. Obviously, he was lucky to have the highly trained and experienced Macedonian army and skilled officers behind him, and he must have had a superb intelligence corps and commissariat. Because our sources focus on the king himself, these unsung heroes tend to be ignored, but without a highly developed infrastructure the huge army would have starved to death before getting far into Asia. His notions of invincibility were reinforced by spectacular military successes in set battles, siege warfare, and guerrilla tactics. Alexander led from the front and, although this was undoubtedly an inspiration to his troops, he took foolhardy risks. On more than one occasion he was lucky not to have been killed. The successive wounds which he endured must have contributed to his demise by increasing his susceptibility to the fever which killed him.

What about Alexander the man? We have no reason to suppose that he did not love his wife Rhoxane, nor that he did not take his pleasures with other women when he wished. His close friendship with Hephaistion may indicate that he was bisexual, but this was a common trait among men in ancient Greece. He rewarded loyalty, punished suspected treachery, and became increasingly autocratic in his treatment of people. Many scholars have claimed that he became a virtual tyrant by the end of his life. He had a court sculptor, portrait painter, and gem engraver to ensure that he was depicted in the correct image. Clearly it was important that an identifiable likeness of him was recognisable by the many peoples of his far-flung empire, but such a conscious manipulation of his image indicates considerable vanity. It is not a coincidence that the extant ancient portraits of Alexander are easily recognisable. They all feature an upturned gaze with consequent wrinkled forehead, eyes deep-set apparently to show fixed determination, and thick leonine locks falling from a peak in the centre of his forehead (see plates 1–3, 11 and 12).

Much has been made of Alexander's drinking habits. Certainly the consumption of wine played a large role at court banquets, festivals, victory celebrations, and around the campfire, and it must have been a considerable consolation during long winters spent in unspeakable conditions far from home. Drinking was an accepted part of Macedonian aristocratic society and army life, and we should not see it as something out of the ordinary. It appears that Alexander drank more as he got older, and that his personality deteriorated during the years of the campaign, whatever may be the reason for this. Nor do we have any reason to doubt the various monumental drinking binges which are recorded in the sources, most famously the one which exacerbated his final illness. Clearly the influence of alcohol had occasional catastrophically detrimental effects on Alexander – his inebriated murder of Cleitus is the most striking example – but I find it hard to believe that he was an alcoholic by the modern clinical definition of the term. His military achievements alone argue that he was in control of his faculties, and more, when he needed to be.

Finally, what were Alexander's views about a divine ancestry, rivalry of the exploits of the gods, and deification? Yet again, these are impossible questions to answer because of our complete lack of evidence about what Alexander himself thought. We have seen that he repeatedly compared himself with the gods Heracles and Dionysus and with Persian heroes such as Cyrus the Great and the legendary Queen Semiramis. He also evidently saw himself in a special relationship with Zeus Ammon after his visit to the oracle at Siwah. His unsuccessful attempt to introduce proskynesis among his Macedonians, and his unclear motives for so doing, have already been discussed. It is certain that Alexander was worshipped as a god after his death (he was worshipped as the 'Founder' god in Egyptian Alexandria, for example), but what is still disputed is whether Alexander demanded divine honours during his lifetime, and, if so, whether he was the first living mortal in the Greek world to do so. We cannot know whether he was intentionally deluding others to increase his stature in their eyes, or whether, in a spectacular case of *folie de grandeur*, he was ultimately deluding himself.

EPILOGUE:
ALEXANDER'S
LEGACY

On 10 June 323 BC, Alexander the Great died of fever in Babylon at the age of thirty-three. According to some accounts, he is alleged to have said on his deathbed, when asked to whom he was leaving his kingdom, 'to the best man'. Some sources add that he gave his signet ring to the general Perdiccas, who was virtually his second-in-command at the time. Most sources relate the further story that Alexander said that there would be a great 'funeral game' over him. This comment – whether real or invented – drips with considerable irony. Equestrian and athletic funeral games (in Greek 'epitaphia') were indeed staged as a way of commemorating the dead in ancient Greece, but here of course Alexander is referring proleptically to the bloody contest over his succession. (Diodorus describes the elaborate funeral carriage constructed for Alexander's body; see plate 10).

This prophecy proved all too true. A vast conquered empire, the focus of which had been the personality of Alexander himself, and which was governed only by interim, *ad hoc* administrative arrangements, was unexpectedly left leaderless. The generals in Babylon – self-made men who had become powerful by virtue of their connection with Alexander and who by now were hardly going to be satisfied by the thought of a quiet life back in Macedonia – immediately fell out over the succession. The main party declared Alexander's posthumous half-Bactrian son by Rhoxane as King Alexander IV, while the rank and file of the army proclaimed Alexander's half-witted half-brother Philip Arrhidaeus as King Philip III (Arrhidaeus was the son of Philip II by one of his minor wives). The infant and the simpleton were placed under the control of a regent. The turmoil which followed in the next two decades presents difficulties of nightmarish complexity, with continually shifting alliances among the leading protagonists who struggled for power even as they pretended to protect the rights of the two kings. The fight was between those who thought that they could take Alexander's place and keep his empire intact, and those who were content with control of self-contained segments of that empire. Constant warfare and the violent deaths of various contenders ensued before three separate kingdoms emerged which form the focus of the history of the next three centuries. Ultimately, the impact of Rome's increasing domination of the Greek East by the first century BC put an end to the independent existence of these empires and what is known as the 'Hellenistic' period of Greek history. Alexander's empire, by which I mean the personal empire he created in these years and not the Macedonian state, did not survive his death. In terms of the attempt to control the whole of Greece and Asia, and to create an empire based on his personality alone, Alexander's achievement was ephemeral.

Nor did he leave the legacy of a bloodline. Within thirty years of his death every member of his immediate family had been brutally murdered: his mother, his wife, his child (the teenage Alexander IV is probably the occupant of Tomb III at Vergina) is probably the occupant of Tomb III at Vergina), an alleged illegitimate son, his half-brother Arrhidaeus, his two half-sisters and the daughter of one of them, and his full sister. This is comment enough upon those troubled years which saw the extinction of the royal Argead family to which Alexander belonged. Most of the surviving generals (the so-called 'Diadochi' or 'Successors') were killed in battles against each other, so no Macedonian dynasty of kings over the whole of Asia was created. It was only after fifty years of chaos that Antigonus Gonatas, the grandson of one of Alexander's generals, securely established himself upon the throne of Macedonia itself, thereby beginning what is known as the Antigonid dynasty in that kingdom. No descendant of Alexander had previously lived to occupy this throne for more than a few years.

Finally, what was the significance of Alexander's expedition in the history of the ancient world? On the one hand, it is undeniable that his exploits brought him everlasting fame and made him a yardstick against which many later conquerors measured themselves – Julius Caesar, the Roman emperor Trajan, and even Napoleon, to name but three. Alexander died at the pinnacle of his fame, and thereby became the quintessential romantic figure. Legend has immortalised him as the consummate young, brave, swashbuckling, invincible hero, but his early death means that we can never know what might have happened later. Could he have held his empire together? How would he have ruled it? Did he really intend the megalomaniac so-called 'Last Plans' recorded in some of our sources, which even included the circumnavigation of Africa? (The authenticity of these plans, which were read out to the army and rejected after Alexander's death, is still hotly debated.) Might he have gone on to conquer the whole inhabited world? Could he really have crossed China and reached the Pacific Ocean? What would Alexander have been like at the age of sixty? We will never know.

There are two legacies which Alexander the Great did bequeath to us, the value of both being dubious. The first was the subsequent condition of Macedonia, which he left as a youth of twenty and to which he never returned. This kingdom had to endure for eleven years with an absent king, far away and in only sporadic contact. It has been estimated that up to 40,000 men in their prime were taken out of Macedonia between 334 and 331 BC. Most of these never returned; many of those who had not succumbed to their wounds lived and died in Asia, populating the new cities founded by Alexander's successors in their new kingdoms. The consequences of this upon the Macedonian families – parents, wives, children – of these soldiers can hardly be imagined. Macedonia was supreme and invincible at the end of the reign of Philip II in 336 BC, but Alexander died leaving behind him bitter memories of brothers, husbands and sons who went with him, and the consequences of severe depopulation. One might argue that Alexander the Great, the greatest conqueror of the ancient Greek world, set his country on a path of decline that proved irreversible. In terms of the Macedonian heartland, the period of Macedonian greatness was the reign of King Philip II, not that of his over-ambitious heir.

John Keegan, the eminent military historian, has examined various styles of generalship in his magisterial book *The Mask of Command*. His definition of the 'mask of command' is the facade or persona which any general must wear, or the stage upon which any leader must act, to ensure that his troops follow him to the end. His discussion of Alexander the Great concludes that his style of leadership combined the ideals of heroism and nobility with that of the 'conquering urge', a savagery which all those who opposed him faced. Keegan's conclusion, with which I wholly concur, is that Alexander's 'dreadful legacy was to ennoble savagery in the name of glory and to leave a model of command that far too many men of ambition sought to act out in the centuries to come'.* It is that legacy which we have inherited.

* John Keegan, *The Mask of Command*, London, Jonathan Cape, 1987, p. 91.

BIBLIOGRAPHY

Bieber, M. *Alexander the Great in Greek and Roman Art*, Chicago, Argonaut, 1964

Bosworth, A.B. *Conquest and Empire. The Reign of Alexander the Great*, Cambridge University Press, 1988

Briant, Pierre *Alexander the Great*, London, Thames and Hudson, 1996

Engels, D.W. *Alexander the Great and the Logistics of the Macedonian Army*, Berkeley, Los Angeles and London, University of California Press, 1978

Ginouvès, René (ed.) *Macedonia from Philip II to the Roman Conquest*, Athens, Ekdotike Athenon, 1993

Green, Peter *Alexander of Macedon 356–323 BC. A Historical Biography*, Berkeley, Los Angeles and London, University of California Press, 1991 (1974)

Hamilton, J.R. *Alexander the Great*, London, Hutchinson University Library, 1973

Hammond, N.G.L. *Alexander the Great: King, Commander, and Statesman*, Bristol, The Bristol Press, 3rd edn, 1994

—— *The Genius of Alexander the Great*, Chapel Hill, The University of Carolina Press, 1997

Hammond, N.G.L. and Walbank, F.W. *A History of Macedonia*, Vol. III (336–167 BC), Oxford, Clarendon Press, 1988, Part 1

Bibliography

Lane Fox, Robin *Alexander the Great*, London, Futura Publications, 1973

—— *The Search for Alexander*, Boston and Toronto, Little, Brown, 1980

Lewis, D.M., Boardman, J., Hornblower, S. and Ostwald, M. (eds) *The Cambridge Ancient History,* Vol. VI (The Fourth Century BC), Cambridge University Press, 1994, chapters 14–17

Milns, R.D. *Alexander the Great*, London, Hale, 1968

Sekunda, Nick *The Army of Alexander the Great* (Osprey Men-at-Arms Series, no. 148), London, Osprey Publishing, 1984

Wilcken, U. *Alexander the Great*, London, Chatto and Windus, 1932; expanded edn with Eugene N. Borza, New York and London, W.W. Norton, 1967

POCKET BIOGRAPHIES

This series looks at the lives of those who have played a significant part in our history – from musicians to explorers, from scientists to entertainers, from writers to philosophers, from politicians to monarchs throughout the world. Concise and highly readable, with black and white plates, chronology and bibliography, these books will appeal to students and general readers alike.

Available

Beethoven
Anne Pimlott Baker

Mao Zedong
Delia Davin

Scott of the Antarctic
Michael De-la-Noy

Sigmund Freud
Stephen Wilson

Marilyn Monroe
Sheridan Morley and
Ruth Leon

Rasputin
Harold Shukman

Jane Austen
Helen Lefroy

POCKET BIOGRAPHIES

Forthcoming

Marie and Pierre Curie
John Senior

Ellen Terry
Moira Shearer

David Livingstone
Christine Nicholls

Margot Fonteyn
Alistair Macauley

Winston Churchill
Robert Blake

Abraham Lincoln
H.G. Pitt

Charles Dickens
Catherine Peters

Enid Blyton
George Greenfield

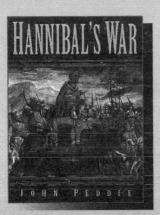